Rowdy Rhinos

GROWING UP WILD

Madison Parker

NorwoodHouse Press

Cataloging-in-Publication Data

Names: Parker, Madison.
Title: Rowdy rhinos / Madison Parker.
Description: Buffalo, NY : Norwood House Press, 2026. | Series: Growing up wild | Includes glossary and index.
Identifiers: ISBN 9781978574205 (pbk.) | ISBN 9781978574212 (library bound) | ISBN 9781978574229 (ebook)
Subjects: LCSH: Rhinoceroses--Infancy--Juvenile literature. | Rhinoceroses--Juvenile literature.
Classification: LCC QL737.U63 P375 2026 | DDC 599.66'81392--dc23

Published in 2026 by
Norwood House Press
2544 Clinton Street
Buffalo, NY 14224

Designer: Rhea Magaro
Editor: Kim Thompson

Photo credits: Cover, p. 1 Corrie Barnard/Shutterstock.com; p. 5 Reinhold Leitner/Shutterstock.com; p. 6 Dave Pusey/Shutterstock.com; p. 7 Ian Murdoch/Shutterstock.com; pp. 8, 9 Juanimal98/Shutterstock.com; p. 10 Thomas Drahos/Shutterstock.com; p. 11 Marie-Anne AbersonM/Shutterstock.com; p. 13 Jonathan Pledger/Shutterstock.com; p. 14 Brester Irina/Shutterstock.com; p. 15 Shuur0172/Shutterstock.com; p. 16 PACO COMO/Shutterstock.com; p. 17 Alan Jeffery/Shutterstock.com; p.18 Udo Kieslich/Shutterstock.com;p. 21 Shams F Amir/Shutterstock.com;

Printed in the United States of America

CPSIA compliance information: Batch #CSNHP26: For further information contact Norwood House Press at 1-800-237-9932.

TABLE OF CONTENTS

Rowdy Rhinos

Rhinos grow up in the **wild**. Baby rhinos are called calves.

How Baby Rhinos Look

Rhino calves are big! They have **wrinkled** gray skin.

They have **hooves** on their feet.

A baby rhino is born with a bump on its head. One day, a **horn** will grow there.

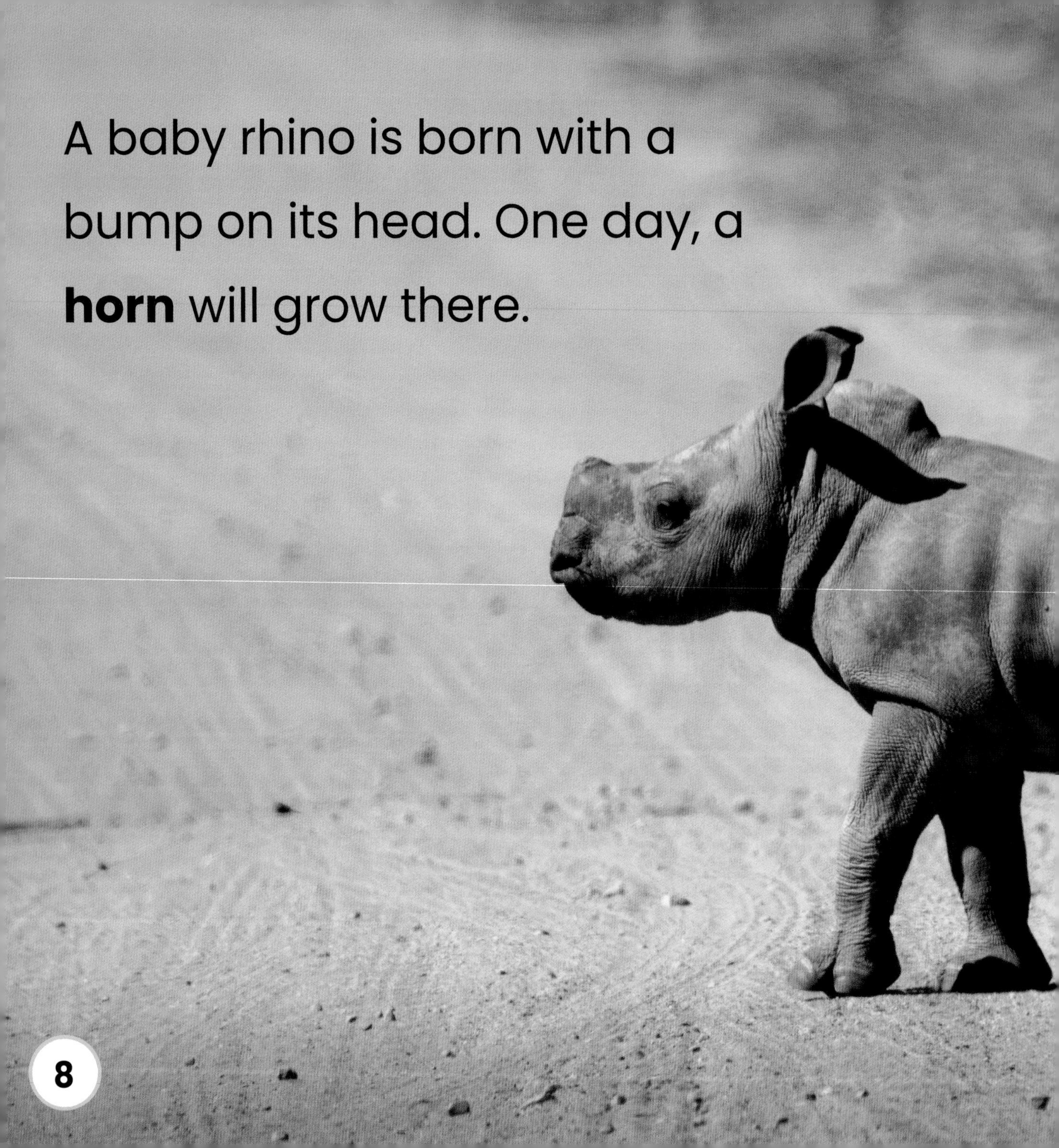

How Baby Rhinos Sound

A group of rhinos is called a crash. Baby rhinos **communicate** with their crash.

Calves coo when they want food. They roar when they are in danger.

What Baby Rhinos Eat

Rhino calves drink their mothers' milk. When they are a few weeks old, they try other foods.

Rhinos are **herbivores**. They eat plants.

As calves grow, they **graze** on grass. They also eat other plants.

Lots to Learn

Baby rhinos can stand right after they are born. Soon, they learn to run.

Rhino calves practice **charging**. This helps them protect themselves.

Baby rhinos learn to **wallow** in mud. This keeps them cool. It keeps bugs away.

All Grown Up

By the time they are five years old, young rhinos are **mature**. Adult females stay with the crash. Males leave to live on their own.

Glossary

charging (CHAHR-jing): attacking in a rush; running forward into something

communicate (kuh-MYOO-ni-kate): to share information and feelings

graze (graze): to feed on grass or plants that are growing in the ground

herbivores (HUR-buh-vorz): animals that eat only plants

hooves (hoovz): hard parts that cover the feet of rhinos, horses, and other animals

horn (horn): a hard, pointed growth on an animal's head

mature (muh-CHOOR): fully grown or developed; adult

wallow (WAH-loh): to roll around in something such as water or mud

wild (wilde): natural places where no people live

wrinkled (RING-kuhld): having small folds and lines

Thinking Questions

1. What are baby rhinos called?

2. Name three body parts that rhinos have.

3. What is a group of rhinos called?

4. What do baby rhinos eat?

5. At what age are young rhinos mature?

Index

About the Author

Madison Parker spent her childhood in the city of Chicago, Illinois. A farm girl at heart, today she lives in Wisconsin with her husband and four children on a small farm with cows, goats, chickens, and two miniature horses named Harley and David. Her favorite dessert is vanilla frozen custard with rainbow sprinkles, even in the winter.